The Essential Steps to Embracing
Your Journey and Loving Your Life

My Dearest Self, I Forgive You

EVE ROSENBERG

© 2023 by Eve Rosenberg

All rights reserved. No part of this book may be reproduced in whole or part, or stored in a retrieval system, with the exception of brief quotations embodied in critical articles or reviews, or transmitted in any form or by any means, electronic, mechanical, photocopying, recording, or otherwise, without the written permission of the author. Requests for permission should be addressed in writing to the author at Eve@lessonslearnedinlove.com.

ISBN: 978-1-7328506-6-8 (Hardcover)
ISBN: 978-1-7328506-7-5 (Paperback)
ISBN: 978-1-7328506-8-2 (eBook)

Library of Congress Control Number: 2023916712

Printed in Delray Beach, Florida, USA by Eve Rosenberg

DISCLAIMER

This book is designed to provide general educational information about the topics discussed and not to diagnose, treat, cure, or prevent any psychological or emotional condition. It is not intended as a substitute for any diagnosis or treatment recommended by the readers' psychiatrist, psychologist, or any other medical practitioner. Use of this book does not establish any doctor-patient relationship between the reader and the author or publisher.

The author does not assume and hereby disclaims any liability to any party for any loss, damage, or disruption caused by errors or omissions, whether such errors or omissions result from accident, negligence, or any other cause. No warranties or guarantees are expressed or implied by their choice of content for this volume and there is no guarantee that these materials are suitable for the reader's particular purpose or situation. If you suspect you have a psychological or emotional problem, we urge you to seek help from the appropriate specialist. This book is not intended to be a substitute for the advice of a licensed physician or mental health provider.

Readers must rely on their own judgment about their circumstances and take full responsibility for all actions and decisions made because of reading this book and applying the recommended practices.

The author has made every effort to ensure the accuracy of the information within this book was correct at the time of publication. Any perceived slights of specific persons, peoples, or organizations are unintended. All names have been changed and any reference to a specific story or instance is coincidental.

For more information, visit Eve Rosenberg at www.howtobelieveinyou.com.

*For Tabitha, my fur baby and soulmate.
You spent your life in awe of me and I of you.
You were the gentlest, purest soul. Thank you for
the blessing of loving you profoundly.*

*For my beautiful, inner child, Evie. This book
is for you, for us, and for all we endured along
our journey together. I love you.*

ACKNOWLEDGMENTS

I want to thank everyone I have met on my journey; those I have loved and those I still don't like. You have all played a part in my joy.

To my Publisher, Diana Needham at Business Book Partners, none of my books would exist without your support. I appreciate you beyond.

To my Cover Designer, Nathan Dasco, and my Book Designer, Amit Dey, thank you for bringing my vision to life. My deepest appreciation.

To Rich Dellamorte, thank you for your attention to every detail. Your final review polished my words and made them shine even brighter.

To all the courageous people who stay true to themselves, I salute you. And to those with big regrets, you deserve to forgive yourself and heal. Be happy.

A NOTE TO THE READER

Whenever I desire to spark positive change in my life, I gravitate toward practices and how-to guides. As much as I appreciate teaching memoirs chock-full of the Author's advice, inspiring stories about themselves and others, I find that these supportive gems lose their usefulness after some time, ending up on shelves or getting donated to charities.

Since self-forgiveness is a daily practice, a process that spans a lifetime and requires consistency and focused attention, I imagined a keepsake, a book one dare not part with, not to be overly dependent on, but instead to trust as a go-to guide for instant comfort, inspiration and directed action. I envisioned this book with a simple, yet bold cover, whose title captured the intended meaning, that spoke volumes to the person seeing it, where *I could use some of that*, would be felt in the gut. I thought of this book as being available and accessible at arm's length, housed on a nightstand, coffee table, or Kindle. My favorite being the hard-covered version because there is nothing better than holding a well-made book in my hands. So, I got busy creating it.

Voila! Here it is!

My Dearest Self, I Forgive You is that trustworthy guide that has limitless potential. The wisdom within is for you to ponder, the suggested action steps are yours to partake in, all in your own time and at your own will. The hope, from my Dearest Self to your Dearest Self, is that you choose to set yourself free.

WHY SELF-FORGIVENESS? WHY NOW??

The profound path ahead, should you commit to forgive yourself, will support you in becoming your sacred admirer, best friend, trusted confidante, and healthy skeptic so you protect yourself at all costs.

Letting your guard down is not encouraged in this book. I feel strongly that being guarded is essential and wise. I wish I had known this back when I blindly trusted everyone without question. Instead, I followed the guidance I was taught, the direction I was given, the quiet voice in my head nudging me, *people are counting on you to do the right thing.* It was predictable I would comply without thinking or resisting, a red flag many of us salute at attention. Either way, this posed no threat to forgiving myself because I made the decision to play Full Out. Giving everyone the benefit of the doubt got added to my list of things to forgive myself for.

It was imperative I write this book solely about self-forgiveness and not about forgiving others. I have faith many of us would welcome a much-needed break from having to wish our offenders well. Since I am a firm believer that God forgives all, and Karma spares no one their lessons, I don't need to concern myself with people who don't deserve my time and energy, especially the people I have experienced big betrayals with. I feel more empowered when I forgive myself and trust that The Universe takes care of the rest. I do, however, thank everyone involved, especially my offenders, because their lessons were essential for my growth. *Merci beaucoup!*

If you are willing, receive this book as a call and reminder to take charge of your life and to live it as you intend. You are the only one who can change your life to suit your needs, desires, and dreams.

In addition to making a commitment to forgive ourselves, we must stop adhering to the conditioning that deems us a sacrificial lamb for another's taking, for the sake of others, for the *Collective* or *Greater Good* we've been chanting about. Because if we continue marching down this road at the accelerated pace we have been going, discounting the *individual*, we will end up a group of exhausted, miserable, angry resisters who won't have any desire to help ourselves or each other out. How does that make for a worthy *Collective* or *Greater Good*? Let's wake up and smell the animosity. Most of us are angry and we have the right to be! We are burdening each other while disrespecting the individual self; and therefore, we lose genuine connection with ourselves and others. There is nothing to gain and everything to lose in such a toxic dynamic. Do you ever wonder who benefits from the totality of all of us, if none of us count? Does this make any real sense to you? I conclude that it only benefits those that are setting the rules that we readily follow. We must say no.

Once we accept that we count, that we are important and that we are entitled to a happy, full life on our terms, we will become more generous and giving. It is only when we are filled up that we not only choose to give, but we also yearn to contribute. Who doesn't want to leave a legacy behind?

My Dearest Self, I Forgive You is meant to lift you out of your People-Pleasing ways and get busy with loving and honoring you, while forgiving yourself for not doing this sooner. To earn the privilege and honor to serve others, you must stop abusing the one person that must count most in your life: You. There is no better time than now to reset your priorities and reclaim your worth. At the end of the day, it doesn't matter how many people you support. If you are neglecting yourself, you are not being kind, and you won't be genuine with others.

If you are ready to get the love and respect that you want and deserve, self-forgiveness is the path you must walk. It is in this journey where you not only claim your worth, but you also declare it. The sooner you forgive yourself for everything and anything you hold against you, the sooner your best life begins.

This book is intended to be a compassionate slap in the face to support you in waking up to your greatness. It is time to get busy living your intended life.

Only you can set yourself free.

INTRODUCTION

Toward the latter part of 2019, I was busily writing away without a care in the world, other than to share some useful wisdom I had accumulated over the years about the breakdown of my relationships. Adding to that mix, thirteen years of coaching clients who suffered substantial heartache, I had a pretty good idea of what we all had in common.

What was to be my fourth book, *Nice Guy, Not So Nice, How to Turn Heartache into Wisdom and Get the Love You Want*, a teaching memoir I believed would earn its rightful place in the self-improvement genre, told of my marriage to a narcissist with a convincing *nice guy* persona, who resorted to mind games and gaslighting to get his way with things. Instead, he became the catalyst that woke me up to my truth: I was living a lie. My intention for readers was to summon up the willingness and courage to see their challenges in a new light too, and to make sense of their experiences while using their newfound wisdom to proactively take charge of their lives and relationships.

And then unexpectedly, after celebrating the holidays, ringing in the new year and preparing for spring, more specifically, in March of 2020, I quickly lost interest in the subject matter of romance gone bad, and knew I had bigger fish to fry. And, because I consider myself to be a woman who walks her talk, I needed the time to go through an initiation on my own, where what once made sense no longer did, and what I once believed to be true about my life and the world was challenged. I had a lot of questions surrounding the darker side of humanity and wondered whether I had been right all along, when I sensed that many of us aren't living our intended lives. Instead, we sacrifice what is important to us for someone else's needs and desires, and how our society applauds it, even though behind closed doors we feel angry and confused.

Regaining my balance after reeling from a traumatic experience much like a mind-f**k of epic proportion, where fear is ever-present, I was reminded that it was me who chose to be clueless for years when it came to important world issues, blindly trusting authority and preferring to remain in the safety of the pink bubble I sheltered myself in, leaving all the responsibility to others. Now, I was forced to open my eyes to things I'd rather not see.

Calling in a vision of what my future might look like, I now desired to take full responsibility and become my greatest advocate and trustworthy ally. I may have faltered during this period, but today I am standing stronger, taller, empowered. Isolation can either put us in a deep depression or get us out of a dependent pattern for good. I'm celebrating the latter. I didn't need to heal my aloneness after all, I needed to love it.

These past three years have inspired me to write this book with urgency. I feel compelled to warn you to take charge of your life, to live it as you, to become an advocate for yourself, and to stop making choices for *them*, because of *them*, despite *them*, whoever *they* are; because, when you do, there is a big price to pay. We may think it's others we fear, or what we will lose if we don't do what we are told to do, or be who *they* want us to be, but I believe strongly that our biggest loss and greatest fear is living with our own wrath in a life we didn't choose.

We are meant to connect with others and healthy relationships are crucial to our happiness, but we must consider the connection with ourselves first. If we continue to leave ourselves out, we are no good to anyone. We can only give that which we have to offer. I assure you that once you are kinder to yourself, you will serve others in ways you cannot imagine now.

I am a believer in the power of saying no. And when we don't, we must forgive ourselves and bow out the next time we feel it in our gut. We must stop betraying ourselves. A life that is lived inauthentically will feel empty and meaningless, much like an emotional death. Without purpose, we blindly feel our way through a fog.

Self-forgiveness is essential for self-love, and yet many of us experience only glimpses of how powerful it is to surrender to our own compassion. Self-forgiveness takes on a debacle that when understood helps things run smoothly. It is also a practice that requires consistency and commitment.

If you want to see clearly, you must remove your blinders and play Full Out.

The Self-Forgiveness Debacle
It took some time and lots of challenges for me to recognize why forgiving myself didn't stick like I hoped it would when I took it on in the past. It was evident in the experiences I was attracting, and the strategies I adopted to deal with them. The arduous path of settling up with myself around all the things I deemed wrong seemed to become more of an uphill battle with time. The mistakes I swore I would never repeat, the habits I committed to break for good, the promises to myself I vowed to not falter on. It all fell by the wayside before it had a chance to make any impact. Forgiving myself seemed an unlikely prospect and had a downside too. After all, how many times can you let

yourself down before you lose all trust, lock the door and throw away the key?

It would make sense to cut ourselves some slack, but in reality, we use all the *get out of jail free* cards for other people we grant the benefit of the doubt to, who we give more than second chances to, who we hope with all hope they will see we are special and love us, and we exert all our energy when it comes to forgiveness on them. It would seem logical and compassionate that when life throws us a curve ball, whether it's a small disappointment or a huge betrayal, that we would step up on our behalf to deliver the tender loving care we are desperate for. But instead, we either beat ourselves up, or crawl into a fetus position on a cold bathroom floor and feel abandoned. And if we are blessed enough to be in the moment and wake up, while most times we don't, we will recognize that this is a fertile time to heed the call. We yearn for our own love and acceptance.

If we are willing to use our heartache as an opportunity to grow and discover our worth, a big step forward, we fail to recognize that a monkey wrench gets thrown into the mix that often sabotages our efforts and holds us back. I wasn't aware of it until I got busy writing this book and woke up in the middle of the night blown away by the insight. Processing our pain and enriching our experiences by seeing the *good* that came out of the *bad*, the *right* out of the *wrong*, has us also wake up to significant bouts of blaming, shaming, and self-loathing, even if it is at a subconscious level. We may not see it or say it out loud, but we feel it deep inside. *If it weren't for my stupid, unlovable, worthless, not good enough self, this wouldn't be happening to me, and I wouldn't have to put a positive spin on things to feel better.* We take inventory of the ways we screwed things up, and contemplate the things we should have, would have, or could have done differently. These revelations can throw us back out into the world, people-pleasing our way to win others' approval, once again avoiding the daunting task of having to accept ourselves for all that we are.

No need to fret. I have developed a simple practice to help assuage self-resentment and it has worked for me like a charm. And, since self-forgiveness is not a one-size-fits-all remedy but an ongoing practice that requires tweaking and tailoring, allow me to introduce it here, so that when you peruse the book, you can keep it in mind for any resentments that come up for you. I have faith you will find this practice helpful provided you use it as instructed and with the intention of success.

I encourage you to approach self-forgiveness with curiosity and compassion for all you have endured and for the exciting future that awaits you.

Set the intention to make this an interesting adventure.

Letting Go of Self-Resentment is a Practice

Imagine that instead of judging your experiences in hindsight, you take a trip back in time to discover your ingenuity and brilliance at the time you made your choices.

Whether you know it or not, whatever drove you to make the choices you made at the time you made them, had a strong impact based on who you were then, the guidance you were given, the conditioning you integrated, your patterns of thought, and the commitments you leaned toward.

Back then, you thought you had the power to change things, had eons of time to get things done and the imagination to believe things would turn out fine. To some extent, you were spot on. You certainly have the power to impact change, your imagination is your greatest asset, but unfortunately, eons of time belong to the fantasy mindset of youth.

Imagine, for example, that you grew up in a family that believed you should marry young and raise a family. You likely adopted that belief even when you felt strongly that it wasn't your path. You may have chosen to go ahead with a wedding you had anxiety about assuring yourself it was *cold feet*, when the real reason was that you didn't want to disappoint everyone. Putting your feelings on the backburner seemed like the right thing to do at the time. You became a People-Pleaser because it seemed like a peaceful option. Then, in hindsight, when you divorced fifteen years later and two children in, you concluded it was the wrong choice, that you weren't happy, that you missed opportunities or cheated yourself. But if you were to go back through a time machine, you would likely make the same choice. Remember, you cannot take your older, wiser self with you. And insecurities have a way of taking precedence in our decision-making process. We usually don't realize we are living a lie until we are deep in because we spend a lot of time and energy convincing ourselves that things will get better, that it's hard to start over, that we can't make it on our own. This keeps us from seeing our options clearly.

And it is likely for some who brilliantly sabotage opportunities when getting close to achieving them, to save themselves from disaster, to then make an about-face, exhausting all avenues to get *there*, even though *there* is what they dread and what they will likely continue to pursue. It is an ego-driven process that sets us up, repeating patterns based on our deep conditioning and the limiting beliefs we hold about ourselves.

I believe the difference lies between the head and the heart. If the desire is our truth and is heart-driven, we will go after that desire with vengeance if we must.

We will do backflips to manifest the resources we need and put forth all effort toward the steps we must take. The *should* desires, instead, lead us astray, not out of fear of failure or success, but out of preservation. Our heart knows the truth even if the ego keeps us engrossed in the same mind games it plays.

Once you forgive yourself for the things you hold over your head, you will hear your heart more clearly. It will speak to you, in its loving whisper, and if you listen closely, you will discover your truth and be led to the right path for you.

In the meantime, you must forgive yourself for all you did not know, and for all you knew and chose not to know.

A Formula to Support Letting Go

I have created a formula that has worked like a charm for me when it comes to letting go of the strikes I hold against myself. When I connect the dots and make sense of things, my curiosity is piqued, and I enjoy learning more about why I do what I do, especially when it comes to my sabotage patterns. After some soul-searching, I was flabbergasted to learn that most of my choices were not my own, but instead influenced by people I either admired or feared. In fact, I revealed a deeply held belief that I had no choice. WOW!

I believe we get blindsided when pursuing what we say we want, when it is what we deeply don't want, are terrified of, that has us sabotage the very opportunities that can lead us to success. We feel conflicted because we don't understand that we are more committed to not getting what we say we want, even when we've convinced ourselves that we do want it, profess to it, and are convinced in our belief in it. This may sound confusing, but I feel certain that fear of success is not an issue at all. Going after something and getting it when deep down the heart doesn't want it, is the bigger failure, the bolder lie, because it complicates matters further by having to maintain an image and status quo of something that was undesirable in the first place.

What if we become more focused on avoiding what we don't want rather than progressing toward what we do want? And, what if what we say we want is what we really don't want? Confused yet?

It may seem scary to look at this, but I can assure you, it is exciting too. Because once you discover the patterns you are stuck in, you can take measures to get unstuck. And, you will have awareness about how you operate, and this is essential in going after any goals you set.

Once you forgive yourself for whatever it is that ails you, the light will come through and you will see things differently than you do now. When you connect to how your experiences come together to produce certain outcomes, how your patterns have been utilized to protect you, and how your commitments are more about what you are avoiding than what you want, you will be able to turn it around to serve you. Keep using this formula whenever you feel a grudge or resentment come up. When you accept a situation you previously rejected because you didn't see the experience as part of a greater outcome, you will appreciate its contribution.

PAST INGENUITY (+) WISDOM EARNED (+) FEEL GOOD STRATEGIES (+) TRIAL AND ERROR = LETTING GO

Past Ingenuity – Regarding the resentment you want to process and heal, go back in time to find the ways you used creative genius in getting what you needed at the time. If you start getting excited about how you manipulated things to serve you, even if it wasn't in your best interest, but instead what you were most committed to at the time, you will discover how powerful you are. Keep in mind that most often we lean toward choices that keep us safe or provide instant gratification.

Wisdom Earned– Regarding this resentment, look for the lessons that it delivered. We didn't realize the stove was hot until we touched it. What do you now know and how can it support you in the future?

Feel Good Strategies – What do you reach out for to feel better? Consider that even for the times when we engage in things that are not good for us, the intention is likely to feel better. Does someone who wants to feel better deserve a beating? Maybe a compassionate heartfelt bonding with oneself would bode better? We tend to lean toward that which makes us feel better rather than facing the music and feeling the pain. Many of our choices are evidence of this.

Trial and Error – How are we supposed to know something until we give it a try? If it doesn't work out in our favor, isn't that good information? Don't you want to know before you invest lots of time, money, and heart? Reconsider the way you think about failing or losing. If you are willing, you will discover that the process of elimination is the best way to discover who you are and what you want. NEXT!

EXAMPLE:

Self-Resentment: I am angry at myself for marrying that guy, I wasted the prime years of my life, never had the children I wanted, and screwed myself in the divorce settlement.

Past Ingenuity: At the time I agreed to move forward with this marriage, I stepped over a lot of things that didn't feel right, but I also believed I was getting a lot out of it too. In fact, I worked diligently to get this guy to marry me and even left him at one point, giving him an ultimatum. I did whatever I could at the time to imagine a great outcome and saw a lavish life ahead. For a good while, I was super excited he wanted to marry me. And our families were cheering for us. There were some good times too. I was very insecure back then and believed I couldn't take care of myself. Even so, I honed an 'I've got it all together' persona. It helped to convince even me that I would make things okay. It takes brilliance, ingenuity, and skill to carry out our fantasies.

Wisdom Earned: Even though the marriage wasn't a good one and led to divorce, I learned so much about what I didn't want in a relationship and gained some confidence in myself.

Feel Good Strategies: While I was concerned about marrying him, I wanted to be married. I wanted to start my life in my home with someone I loved and have a family. I went ahead with the marriage because I thought it would make me happy. When it didn't work out and I grieved for the end of my marriage, I ate a lot, drank too much, started therapy, and didn't date for a long time. I was in a lot of pain and did some things I wasn't proud of. All my actions seemed likely for someone who had dreams that fell apart. Back then I believed they were my dreams. When we don't know ourselves well, we guess a lot. I became depressed.

Trial and Error: If I hadn't married him, I would have always wondered. I'm sure I would have beat myself up if I'd let him get away. I couldn't have known the outcome even with the red flags I ignored. I was young and naïve at the time. I gave it a try. Is that a good reason to keep beating myself up?

Conclusion: Using this formula to examine resentment brings clarity and makes it more attractive to let resentments go because it examines the experience to find the good things that came out of the pain and heartache. Making sense of things heightens our willingness to keep exploring and helps to bring compassion to the self. It facilitates moving on. It is the win in the loss.

FROM MY DEAREST SELF TO YOUR DEAREST SELF,

I hope you set yourself free.

Self-forgiveness isn't about wiping the slate clean.

It is about **making sense of the mess** and loving yourself despite it.

XO *Take a step forward on your behalf:*

Examine a negative experience in your life that you are still holding on to. Use the Self-Resentment Formula on the previous page to examine the situation and find some good in it.

Even when we screw things up, we do so with **brilliance** and **ingenuity**. Don't underestimate your skills.

Sabotage is not an easy feat. It takes determination and skill just like it does to go after our goals.

XO *Take a step forward on your behalf:*

Write a paragraph about how brilliantly you have sabotaged an opportunity in your life and consider how you went about it. Imagine how successful you will be once you utilize your brilliance and ingenuity to serve you.

If I was falling off a cliff and had one sentence to shout out to the world before I crashed and died, it would be:

LOOK TO HOW OTHERS TREAT YOU AND YOU WILL KNOW HOW YOU FEEL ABOUT YOURSELF!

When you change how you see yourself and treat yourself better, others will follow your lead.

XO *Take a step forward on your behalf:*

Always remember this. Never forget it. Obsessively use it as a mantra. Write it anywhere and everywhere so you are reminded of this truth.

To make a promise is to break a pattern.

MEAN IT – Make the commitment.

MEAN UP – Say NO! Be firm. Set Boundaries.

MEAN WELL – Set good intentions that are positive and serve you.

MEAN BUSINESS – Follow through.

XO *Take a step forward on your behalf:*

Stop betraying yourself. Start now. Following the above strategy, make a promise to yourself.

We either see ourselves as a **BLESSING** or a **BURDEN**, and we treat ourselves accordingly.

Which are you?

It is natural to avoid a burden.

When it comes to **burdens**, we will procrastinate

'til the cows come home.

Don't wait for the cows. Declare yourself a **blessing** now.

Fake it 'til you feel it.

XO *Take a step forward on your behalf:*

Treat yourself as if you are a blessing. We treat our blessings with love and care.

This is an essential daily practice for self-forgiveness.

You won't magically wake up one morning in love with yourself, but you can go to bed at night with more admiration than you had the day before.

XO *Take a step on your behalf:*

Admire yourself. Admire yourself. Admire yourself some more. The warm and fuzzy feelings will catch up. Count your skills and qualities that you are proud of.

ENOUGH IS MORE.

Instead of using your efforts and energy to become better than you are, be where you are and celebrate that you are enough.

XO *Take a step on your behalf:*

Buy yourself something expensive that you have been wanting.

Enough deserves plenty.

You determine how worthy you are.
Don't grant others that privilege.

Forgive yourself for informing others that they needn't go out of their way for you.

XO *Take a step forward on your behalf:*

Throw a party for no reason other than to celebrate with you, The Guest of Honor.

Indicate on the invite that *Gifts are welcome and appreciated.*

RIGHT YOUR STORY

You read that right.

Right your story.

XO *Take a step forward on your behalf:*

When you stop making things wrong, you will be *right*ing your story. Look for the blessings and write a one-page synopsis of your life presented as a blessing.

If you truly want to be seen by others for all that you are, leave your diary out on the coffee table for everyone to read.

Yeah, I didn't think so.

The only person that needs to *get you,* is you.

Once you fall in love with yourself you will get this.

XO *Take a step forward on your behalf:*

Speak highly and proudly of yourself in the presence of others, and don't apologize for getting teary-eyed when you are blown away by how inspiring you are.

Make it a habit to enjoy your own company.

By yourself, with yourself.

Bond.

XO *Take a step forward on your behalf:*

Schedule a date night with yourself and do something you love.

Boundaries speak louder than hugs.

Avoiding confrontations doesn't make for authentic harmony. There are times when difficult conversations take precedence over making up.

XO *Take a step forward on your behalf:*

Have a conversation with someone you need to set a boundary with. You will be angry at yourself for putting it off. Self-forgiveness requires fulfilling your emotional needs.

If you don't say **NO**, you will hear it a lot.

Others are teaching you the **POWER OF CHOICE**.

Stop enabling them to use and disrespect you.

We teach people how to treat us.

XO *Take a step forward on your behalf:*

Say no without the back story. The more you explain, the greater chance others will plead with you to get their way, and you will likely betray yourself by backing down. To forgive yourself and take yourself seriously, you must keep your word.

If you refuse the remedy, then accept that you choose to remain sick. No one is coming to save you. You must act on your own behalf.

There are signs and messages anywhere, everywhere, all around you, all the time, never-ending guidance at your disposal.

Sitting around whining, believing you have no options, and doing nothing about a situation you are miserable in, will inform The Universe that you are settling on remaining a victim.

Make a new choice. Climb out of your rut.

XO *Take a step forward on your behalf:*

Take a baby step. They count.

Give yourself time to forgive yourself while timing yourself.

Forgiving yourself is a process and a practice.

Play **FULL OUT**.

Self-forgiveness must become a part of your daily routine.

 *Take a step forward on behalf of you:*

Make a list of all the things you want to forgive yourself for. Take a deep breath and give yourself a hug. Now is the time for compassion, not complaints. Take the shortcut by doing an honoring action step every day, something that makes you feel special.

A mantra that works every time, in every way, just by saying it.

THANK YOU!

XO *Take a step forward on your behalf:*

Say "Thank you" obsessively and silently to yourself throughout the day, no matter what happens, and especially after kicking and screaming. Just try it. You will be amazed.

You have hurt others. Forgive yourself.

Along with forgiving ourselves for the resentments we hold about ourselves, we also get weighed down by the transgressions we inflict on others.

We must forgive ourselves despite whether we are forgiven by the people we have hurt, despite where we are to blame and despite whether we intentionally meant to inflict pain.

Keep in mind that making amends can and do backfire.

Sure, it feels good to relieve ourselves of guilt and access our kindness. But it can also open a pandora's box and rehash a situation that is best left alone.

 *Take a step forward on your behalf:*

In the safety of your mind, visit some people by using your imagination who you want to apologize to. Allow yourself to make amends for three people you have hurt, to let go of the guilt that has been weighing you down and holding you back. This way, nobody gets hurt further, especially you.

If you keep leaving yourself out to please everyone, you will feel as if you don't belong. It's not about fitting in or standing out, it's about including yourself on your 'make them happy' list.

XO *Take a step forward today on your behalf:*

Make yourself happy today.

A Little Romance, A Lot of Aggravation.

When Jack met Jill, he was over-the-hill infatuated with her. He saw all the light and good things about her. Her beauty captivated him, and he blushed when she laughed at his jokes, the sort of funny anecdotes that many others found odd and obnoxious.

Jill was attracted to Jack's confidence and how he became successful at the young age of thirty-two. He was the middle child between a younger sister and older brother, and his parents were very much in love, as evident in their touchy-feely demonstrations at parties. Jill counted on this as a good sign of things to come.

Shortly after the honeymoon, Jack and Jill quickly realized they had made a big mistake.

Jill was beginning to find Jack's jokes odd and obnoxious, and Jack didn't think Jill was as pretty after gaining twenty pounds overnight.

The divorce was quick and nasty. They didn't speak again.

Moral of the story: Jack didn't like Jack, Jill didn't like Jill, and they played house.

It was all predictable. We must love ourselves to come together and love others.

> Be careful how you interpret romance.
> True love resides within you and for you.
> You must access it on your own.
> It is your approval that you most yearn for.

 Take a step forward on your behalf:

The path to self-love is self-forgiveness. Commit to the process and play Full Out.

We each have an **inner child** within us that yearns for our love and acceptance.

Over time we have grown to dislike them, blame them, and beat them up.

Over time your **inner child** has grown to doubt you, lose trust that you will follow through on your promises, and has shut down communicating their needs and desires with you.

You must first apologize for the neglect and abandonment you have inflicted upon them as well as upon you and choose to replace the criticism with compassion.

Imagine your **inner child** beside you as you navigate life. Make sure, as any **caring** parent would, to look after them, stick up for them, and watch out for them.

From this day forward, you must bond as **one**.

XO *Take a step forward on your behalf:*

Write a letter of apology to your inner child and say you are sorry. Next, write a letter to you from your inner child explaining what they need from you to move forward together in harmony.

If you allow yourself to be angry,
you won't be angry all the time.

You have a right to all your emotions,
and anger is
essential to access your power and passion

FEEL YOUR FEELINGS.

LEARN TO LOVE YOUR ANGER.

IT IS PART OF WHO YOU ARE.

XO *Take a step forward on your behalf:*

What are you angry about? Whatever it is, you have that right. Write about it. It is very healthy to acknowledge and release your anger.

TREAT YOURSELF WELL.

YOU ARE YOUR GREATEST ASSET.

XO *Take a step forward on your behalf:*

What would it look like to treat yourself well? Do it now!

DON'T STEP OUT OF YOUR COMFORT ZONE UNLESS YOU KNOW THE WAY BACK IN.

BE YOUR SOFT PLACE TO FALL.

XO *Take a step forward on your behalf:*

Find at least two ways to comfort yourself.

Hint: Wrap your arms around you in a warm hug, look in the mirror and connect with your eyes. Kiss your hands.

When you least expect it, your expectations will be met.

Since we attract most of our positive experiences when we are in a neutral place; meaning, when we are the least attached to that which we want or expect, we are most likely to receive it.

Wishing, wanting, and hoping are as counterproductive as worrying, fearing, and contemplating a negative outcome.

Here's why:

All of the energetic states I've listed above lack certainty and conviction.

It is in believing something so deeply that we can exhale and become neutral because our trust lies there.

When we believe in ourselves, we are more likely to have faith in the unknown. We feel more capable of handling what comes our way.

When we believe in ourselves, we take a stand for ourselves and sometimes it takes taking that stand to believe more deeply in how worthy we are.

The shortest path toward a neutral, peaceful, energetic state is to forgive yourself because the need to believe in oneself is a prerequisite for grounded faith.

The more I step into forgiveness for myself, the less I am afraid of what lies ahead.

I don't go to bed at night wishing, wanting, or hoping. And my fear and worry has almost diminished.

I have never been more uncertain about my future, while being completely certain and convinced that I will bode well despite what lies ahead.

Self-forgiveness is the safety we yearn for because it allows for bonding with the most important person that is with you to the end: You.

Once you feel your own comfort, love, and compassion, you will feel ten feet taller and able to take on challenges with passion instead of panic.

There is no greater fight worth fighting than the one it takes to see your worth.

Stand at attention and salute the **Red Flags.**

XO *Take a step forward on your behalf:*

Red flags indicate a deep sense of doubt. Don't doubt the doubt.

Take your skepticism seriously.

Follow your **gut**.

Heed your **lessons**.

Throw your **blinders** away.

XO *Take a step forward on your behalf:*

Starting right now, become radically truthful with yourself and don't hide anything. Be the safe space and the safety net that you have been missing.

The strategies you use to win over the people whose forgiveness you seek work very well on the self. **Kiss up** to yourself until you feel warm and fuzzy about you.

It isn't brain surgery. When it comes to forgiving yourself, apologizing isn't going to cut it.

You need to take demonstrative steps to earn your own trust and love, and it takes concentrated effort over time. Here is where it pays to be overly nice. You're so worth it!

 *Take a step forward on your behalf:*

Do something for yourself that makes you feel warm and fuzzy.

**You've left yourself behind
for too long now.
It's time to get in front of the line.**

XO *Take a step forward on your behalf:*

Make yourself your number one priority from now on.

BE WHO YOU ARE, NOT WHO THEY WANT YOU TO BE.

If you're not feeling good enough, aiming to be better doesn't even make sense.

Feelings of inadequacy usually arise from trying too hard to be something you are not.

XO *Take a step forward on your behalf:*

Write in your journal about what you want others to see about you. If someone were to "get you," what would they say?

ASK YOURSELF THE QUESTIONS YOU REACH OUT TO ASK OTHERS. YOU KNOW THE RIGHT ANSWERS.

XO *Take a step forward on your behalf:*

Trust your gut, your intuition, your instincts, common sense.

No one knows what's best for you than you.

Instead of making excuses for why the people you don't like are the way they are, use your energy to give yourself compassion for why you choose to put up with them.

If you are going to surround yourself with people who offend you, have compassion for yourself during the time they misbehave.

If options permit, leave.

XO *Take a step forward on your behalf:*

At your discretion, give offenders in your life their walking papers.

Don't be bullied into forgiving anyone. Leave it to the Karma Gods.

Once you forgive yourself, peace will spread throughout your life, wherever you choose to be.

XO *Take a step forward on your behalf:*

Use all your energy on forgiveness on you.

If you need to make others wrong so you can feel right, you are hiding from something bigger than a debate.

Accept what you resist seeing in yourself and set yourself free.

> *Projections are the best way to recover the lost parts of you. Allow others to remind you where to look.*

XO *Take a step forward on your behalf:*

Choose a person whose behavior you disapprove of and choose two qualities to reflect on.

Example: Hateful and Greedy. Find your expression of these qualities. Resistance is an indication that you reject these parts of yourself. Acceptance of all of you will open the door to much love and compassion for you, which facilitates self-forgiveness. Breathe through it.

DEAL BREAKERS ARE YOUR BEST NEGOTIATORS

They never compromise on you.

XO *Take a step forward on your behalf:*

Never, never negotiate on a deal breaker. You will break your trust in you by doing so.

There is a time to **fight** and a time to **surrender**.

Know the difference and you will master your life.

When you forgive yourself and accept the invitation of deeply knowing and trusting you, you will know what time it is and what to do.

 *Take a step forward on your behalf:*

Follow the guidance you are avoiding because you know it is the right thing to do for you.

The best choice is choosing you.

XO *Take a step forward on your behalf:*

It is self-explanatory. Choose you!

COURAGE

is going against a majority to believe what's in your heart.

XO *Take a step forward on your behalf:*

Only share your opinions with like-minded people.

OWN YOUR PERSPECTIVE

Don't waste your energy where you are not heard.

A lot of our resentment is about not being seen or understood by others.

Know where you are welcome and stay clear where you are not.

 *Take a step forward on your behalf:*

Forgive yourself for the times you diminished your energy defending your position to members of the opposition. Knowing what you know should suffice. Own your perspective.

I used to believe that there was real assurance about things and people.

But the only real **security** comes with **loving** yourself, **believing** in you, and **knowing** that whatever storm lies ahead, you will figure things out because you are a resourceful, powerful, amazing force who stands up for you.

Never underestimate your **POWER**.

XO *Take a step forward on your behalf:*

Say a powerful mantra every time you start to worry. Don't disregard your feelings, but comfort them with a loving mantra: *This too shall pass.*

STOP WORRYING AND START BELIEVING.

Trade in the **"what if's"** for the **"as if's."**

Acting or even just pretending **as if** something you desire has happened, your faith will rise to attract it.

XO *Take a step forward on your behalf:*

Fake it, pretend, make believe, use your imagination to see it and it will be yours.

Never paint a room a color you do not look good in.

Honoring steps are crucial to support self-forgiveness. A huge way to honor yourself is to accentuate your beauty in the surroundings you beautify; not only because you are choosing what you love, but because you deserve to shine.

Allow others to bask in your light.

XO *Take a step forward on your behalf:*

Paint a room or an accent wall your favorite color.

> In a world that is unfair, everyone is fair game.

GUARD YOUR BACK

Being guarded isn't the same as being unapproachable. You can be welcoming while watching your back.

XO *Take a step forward on your behalf:*

Be gracious. Be respectful. Be careful.

WE PROTECT WHO AND WHAT WE LOVE.

And that which we choose to protect, we will learn to love.

CHOOSE YOU!

XO *Take a step forward on your behalf:*

If you haven't yet fallen in love with yourself, protecting yourself will be a big step in that direction. Start now.

Insecure moments bring confidence when you mind your own business.

You don't have to point out the run in your black stockings or the spinach in your teeth, to be yourself. Stop micromanaging your appearance and your presentation.

The confidence we yearn for comes from the liberating experience of loving who we are and just being who we are.

 *Take a step forward on your behalf:*

Leave your self-critiques in your journal and be your greatest admirer.

Soon your entries will be raving about you.

How do you think you got so wise?

THAT'S RIGHT! LIFE IS A SCHOOL!

Letting go of self-resentments piques one's curiosity to learn.

XO *Take a step forward on your behalf:*

Do some soul-searching. You will discover that your biggest lessons have come from your greatest heartache. What are you still resenting?

Haven't you prayed for guidance?
Then stop ignoring your gut!

XO *Take a step forward on your behalf:*

Follow your gut. Listen to your intuition. Heed the guidance that you ask for.

A Practice to quiet a busy mind and shift your thoughts

For anything you feel, you will use a generalized statement followed by the word, "matter."

This is going to assist you in neutralizing your thoughts. I have been so amazed by my success with it, that sometimes I try getting the thought back and it just doesn't stick.

EXAMPLE: I am having a problem falling asleep and I have many thoughts swirling in my mind. The general statement I will say is (either silently or out loud),

"**People** who have a hard time falling asleep **matter**."

If my thought then changes to another thought, i.e., *I have such a busy mind,* or *why can't I stop thinking about what she did?* the statement will move to:

"**People** who have a busy mind and cannot stop thinking and ruminating about what happened, **matter**."

If you become impatient with this exercise:

"**People** who are impatient **matter**.

You continue this process until you feel neutral and relaxed.

The word **People** makes the statement general and not personal, and the word **matter** is a key acknowledgement of worth. **It does not matter one bit whether you believe in the statement, it just works. Why? Who cares! It just works!**

 *Take a step forward on behalf of you:*
Try it, you'll love it!

Each time you reoffend yourself, you negate a lesson.

It's time to break the pattern.

When you find yourself repeating behavior that was hurtful to yourself, stop and take a pause.

 *Take a step forward on your behalf:*

Ask yourself these questions:

Now why would I want to do that to myself again? What have I learned that I already know?

Have a conversation with yourself and be radically honest.

BECOME YOUR SACRED ADMIRER.

Keep the relationship with you sacred and you will come to admire yourself in ways you cannot imagine now.

And since the process of self-forgiveness is a sacred one, vow to never give up on you, for you are with yourself at the start and at the end of your journey. I cannot think of anything more sacred than that.

XO *Take a step forward on your behalf:*

Consider the relationship with yourself the priority in your life. It will not only create a deep bond that will support you to know yourself better, it will lift all your relationships to a higher vibration.

Being kind just to be kind, isn't the kind of kind that's really kind.

It pays to be nice and respectful as much as we can, but being overly nice for appearances' sake won't register as a win to the self and will most likely have you doing favors you'd rather not do.

 *Take a step forward on your behalf:*

Use your energy to be overly nice to yourself and treat others with basic respect.

People will like you when you like you.

Learn to love confrontation.

It's the only way you will express your needs
and wants effectively.

XO *Take a step forward on your behalf:*

Everything gets better with time and practice. We even learn to love things we once dreaded once we see how it serves us. Schedule your confrontation.

How to stop ruminating about others and get refocused on YOU.

Whenever you find yourself in a rumination spiral about someone and what they did, didn't do, could have done, should have done and on and on, it is time to take all that energy and refocus on you.

Say silently or out loud as soon as you find yourself thinking about them:

REFOCUS! And imagine a big bright light over your head that is bathing you in its illumination.

Next, say out loud or silently to yourself:

REFRESH! Ask and answer this question: What am I feeling right now?

(You must answer with feelings, i.e., "I feel sad, I feel angry, I feel frustrated.") If you find yourself going back into the dialogue of them and what they did, you must start over with the first step.

After you've acknowledged your feelings, say out loud or silently to yourself:

REGROUP! Ask and answer this question: What do I need to do for myself right now? Give yourself what you need. Maybe your answer is to give yourself a hug, take a walk, take a warm bath, cook a nice meal.

 *Take a step forward on your behalf:*

Repeat this practice as many times as you need to stop ruminating. Give yourself what you need.

GRAB YOUR UMBRELLA THE RAINY DAYS ARE HERE!

How many rainy days did you save for, promise you'd get to, and didn't follow through?

Now that's something to forgive yourself for.

XO *Take a step forward on your behalf.*

Have a rainy day.

My Dearest Self,

I want to apologize to you for all the ways I hurt you.

I am sorry for neglecting, forgetting, over-looking, abandoning and leaving you to hope that someday others will fight for you because I did not.

You see, it's not only about how I behaved and treated you, but it was also all that I needed you to be. It's what I believed you were missing. Or so I thought. I trusted others when I felt I wasn't good enough, and so I looked to you to be bigger, better, bolder. And I must admit I too thought you could be more. I never stopped comparing, competing, judging, insisting you be smarter, prettier, nicer. More, more, more. I blamed you for everything that went wrong.

I treated you badly because I grew to dislike you and all that you weren't. You weren't enough for what I wanted. And I believed I deserved an apology for getting cheated, passed over, forgotten.

Wow! I see it clearly now. I feel ashamed of how abusive I have been and how much I grew to loathe you. If it wasn't for my "I've got it all together" persona that brought me some real glimpses of happiness and peace, despite the exhausting struggle to maintain the mask, I don't know if I would have had this revelation now.

Hey, how about we forgive each other? I forgive you and you forgive me? It's not a tit for tat, but instead an honest making up. Don't forget, you pulled the wool over your eyes too and helped with the sabotage.

Hey, I have a great idea.

Why don't we just forgive each other? And, if you are willing, I suggest this be the most important rule we follow going forward. I will treat you with love, compassion, and empathy, and, in return, you accept my love and be just as you are. Because I see now that you were always enough, even when you tried so hard to be too much. And me wanting more isn't a crime. No need to punish us any longer.

I am over the moon so proud and grateful. I love you.

My Dearest Self, I forgive you.

MIND YOUR OWN JOURNEY

Your experience of the world is YOURS.

Have faith and trust in your journey. It is uniquely yours. Pack lightly.

XO *Take a step forward on your behalf:*

Make a list of ten things you appreciate about your life and the direction you feel guided to follow.

A Know-it-All knows all it knows because it doesn't care to know what it doesn't want to know.

NEVER CLOSE YOUR MIND TO INFORMATION OF ANY KIND BECAUSE YOU NEVER KNOW WHAT YOU NEED TO KNOW

Always do your due diligence and you will have less regrets in all situations.

XO *Take a step forward on your behalf*:

Don't let anyone tell you the way things are. Listen, but do your own research and follow your gut. There is a lot you know and a lot you don't know.

NEVER TRUST ANYONE COMPLETELY!!!

The operative word is "completely."

XO *Take a step forward on your behalf:*

Never do it with anyone, ever! Remember, the operative word is "completely."

Ideals are unreachable stars best left for gazing on a breezy night.

Striving for unconditional love, even expecting it, is probably the biggest sabotage pattern we've all stuck our foot in, with hopes to assuage the loathing we feel for the unlovable qualities we see in ourselves.

A close runner up that gets the job done splendidly is to accept yourself no matter what you have done or will do.

Your acceptance is precious, sacred, and essential to live a life that is full and happy while owning that you are human and flawed.

You will never love yourself unconditionally. How many attempts are you up to?

Forgiving and embracing yourself, conditionals and all, will suffice quite nicely.

Breathe.

Perfection, by the way, is another ideal. Seek it up in the night sky.

 *Take a step forward on your behalf:*

If you choose to remain idealistic, see yourself as the most magnificent creature that ever lived and love yourself up.

The **truth** may be painful, but having to pretend it isn't so becomes the real struggle.

Don't choose to live a **lie**. It makes the **truth** more unbearable.

Pain becomes stronger with time.

Set yourself free.

XO *Take a step forward on your behalf:*

Commit to being radically honest with yourself. Start now.

NO MORE LIES.

Stop telling yourself the untruths that keep you stuck in a situation where you are miserable. It's not a loving choice.

XO *Take a step forward on your behalf:*

No one is coming to save you. That was another big lie you bought into.

Don't change who you are to stay where you don't want to be.

Trying to fit in where you want to belong may not make you feel welcome, but putting efforts toward staying in a situation you don't want to be in is the most abusive treatment toward the self and it declares you don't deserve what you want.

YOU SET THE BAR.

XO *Take a step forward on your behalf:*

It is not loving to stay in situations you are unhappy in. You may believe you are making the choice that is right, but it is far from the right choice. Reconsider your options.

When the person who has betrayed you reveals the truth about something you'd likely never find out, they use you as a sounding board to relieve their guilt. A second strike against you. Don't take the bait and become their therapist. Make your feelings matter most.

MAKE YOUR FEELINGS MATTER MOST.

XO *Take a step forward on your behalf:*

There are times when we want so much to believe someone we trusted didn't do what they did. When they reveal themselves to you, don't use their "coming clean" as a truce. They are letting you know they are a liar, and they want the assurance of your forgiveness. You have a right to process your feelings and you don't owe anyone a speedy decision. Take care of yourself and process your feelings. Forgive yourself for your part in the charade, even if it was just over-trusting.

THERE IS A REASON FOR EVERYTHING AND A LESSON FOR EVERY REASON.

Heed the Call

XO *Take a step forward on your behalf.*

After you react to whatever happened, it would benefit you to find the reason and the lesson that supports the experience. It is not to frustrate you, but instead to guide you in a deeper process for insight to support your growth in a positive way.

TAKE EVERYTHING PERSONALLY. IT'S ALL FOR YOU!

Who's fooling who? Everything is personal. Your experience is personal. Your relationships are personal. Your perception of the world is personal. Stop trying to make it impersonal.

 *Take a step forward on your behalf:*

Once you make things all about you and accept that your journey is all about you, you won't feel as if you belong nowhere. Growth is personal. Soak it up.

You may try hard not to **judge** others or yourself. But I can assure you, hard as it may be, you will never succeed because you are a human being with an ego. The more effort you put forth to achieve the unattainable, the worse you will feel and the harsher you will **judge**.

You are **judging** this book as you read it. Breathe. Enjoy the experience. It's normal.

(Oooops! Another judgment).

HERE COMES THE JUDGE!

We judge to make sense of things, to process what we see, to conceptualize our experiences.

Compliments are judgments too. Do you plan not to compliment anyone ever again?

The more we accept ourselves as judgmental human beings, the more conscious we will be of how we choose to share our opinions.

 *Take a step forward on your behalf:*

Become a gossip machine in the safety of your own mind and judge, judge, judge.

Have fun with it.

Loss is inevitable.

With every loss will come something of value, even in the greatest of losses. It is never to minimize the loss or grief, but instead to provide the fortitude to continue to go on with life.

Allow time to pass. Invite the signs and messages you are shown to comfort you and your healing will begin.

 *Take a step forward on your behalf:*

Do not push away joy or peace during a time of loss. It presents itself to heal not to shame.

Allow, allow, allow.

STOP CENSORING WHO YOU ARE.

We are complex human beings with many facets and parts that make us whole.

We have qualities we like and ones we dislike and believe we are not.

We are everything, the good and the bad.

**Learn to love what you loathe,
and you will be free.**

XO *Take a step forward on your behalf:*

Don't make anything wrong or censor your behavior in your presence.

We aim to hide from others and censor our behavior, but there is no need in the privacy of your own company. Remove the shame. Self-forgiveness becomes easy when you accept yourself for all that you are.

YOU ARE BETTER THAN YOU THINK AND GREATER THAN YOU BELIEVE.

Your self-image needs a radical makeover.

Watch your thoughts carefully and choose to believe in you.

After all, it was a choice to believe you are not good enough.

XO *Take a step forward on your behalf:*

On a blank canvas in the safety of your mind, paint a new, empowering image of you and carry it with you everywhere you go.

CELEBRATE THE SYNCHRONICITIES IN YOUR DAY.
EVERYTHING IS CONNECTED.

With self-forgiveness, the magic unfolds.

The Universe is guiding you.

Pay attention to the signs and messages.

 Take a step forward on your behalf:

Begin connecting the dots of your experiences, making sense of how things flow into each other and create a deeper meaning. It's not about the details, but instead how they create a deeper meaning and lesson for you to see. This phenomenon is your journey. Live it fully.

Don't use your precious energy remembering what you will never forget.

There is no need to keep rehashing your past.

It is noted.

Tuck it away with an intention to heed its lessons.

XO *Take a step forward on your behalf:*

Use your wisdom not your energy.

How much longer are you willing to be okay with a situation that is not okay?

The feelings we work to suppress, rationalize, justify, and convince ourselves that things aren't so bad, or could be worse, use precious energy that otherwise can lift us up and give us strength.

 *Take a step forward on your behalf:*

Ask yourself how much longer you are willing to stay where you are not happy. Gain clarity.

Betrayals have a way of **sticking like glue.**

When we find ourselves in circumstances we are unhappy in, but choose to endure, we may be forced to make a move when others take a stand on behalf of themselves.

This sort of betrayal hits hard and deep because while you choose to betray yourself, others will follow. It's a double whammy.

XO *Take a step forward on your behalf:*

Stop kicking yourself for the choices you made and give yourself a hug. Your love heals.

THE HORIZON APPEARS BRIGHTEST WHEN YOU UNDERSTAND THE UNIVERSE HAS YOUR BACK.

As you continue to connect how others treat you respective of how you treat yourself, The Universe always has your back.

If you are quiet and compassionate with yourself, you will discover that everything that happens brings you closer to your heart.

 *Take a step forward on your behalf:*

Trust that everything is happening to support you to know yourself better. Make a list of at least two times you were offended and how these experiences contributed to your growth.

If you choose to be a caretaker, make sure you don't leave yourself out and don't do it out of guilt. **It must be a desire of the heart and a willing sacrifice**; otherwise, forgiving yourself will become an uphill battle.

Don't allow your guilt to choose another's interests over yours. You would be blown away with how often others will run toward the highway when considering your interests over theirs.

If you make **choices based on what is perceived to be the right thing to do** because you can't live with yourself if you don't, or will feel guilty for the rest of your days if you do, either way you've screwed yourself.

It is time to live your intended life and you are the only one who will care if you don't.

There are always options.

 Take a step forward on your behalf:

Imagine something happens to you and the person you depend on to care for you chooses not to. Would you choose differently for them? It is important to recognize how we truly feel and what we want before making a life-altering decision. Be honest with yourself. Guilt isn't a loving choice.

Our yearning lies not in being loved, but instead in loving so deeply, we get lost in ourselves. Otherwise, there would be no need for a restraining order to ward off the stalker.

YOU MUST MAKE ROOM TO LOVE

XO *Take a step forward on your behalf:*

My mother once told me, "In every relationship, there is someone being kissed and someone doing the kissing." I never forgot it, and for most of my life I wanted to be kissed. I have learned in my later years, as I surround myself with a small circle of beloved friends and my beautiful fur babies, that my desire is to love deeply. I'll admit that reciprocal love is the only kind where I believe it is possible, and each party must have love for themselves. Find that love. Whether it is with a person, a pet, a hobby. Find that love.

Dogs will love you, honor you, and serve you. But don't think for one second that they don't love themselves.

Don't miss out. Dogs are so lovable and loving. It will warm your heart in ways you cannot imagine.

A pet will teach you how to forgive yourself because they will remind you that there are limitless opportunities to show up with love.

 *Take a step forward on your behalf:*

Get yourself a four-legged teacher and learn about love.

Grief, like a fresh wound, takes time to heal. Take the time.

XO *Take a step forward on your behalf:*

Pick a date to become active again. Remember your time is limited too.

Make sure the people that love you know who your best friend is.

YOU!

XO *Take a step forward on your behalf:*

Take a selfie and make it the wallpaper on your phone. This will remind you who your best friend is.

Self-love means always having to say you're sorry.

Apologies to yourself that are consistent, whether they pertain to the past or the present, are compassionate acknowledgments that convey to the self that you care, that you are important, and that you are respected.

Take a step forward on your behalf:

Make this an on-going practice and you will find that the genuine apologies of others will follow.

**When doing the right thing
for others is doing the
wrong thing for you, you must
make the choice
that supports you because
it is the most genuine,
loving choice for everyone in the end.**

Going with the flow may make you appear flexible and accommodating, but if you are going against your heart or where your gut is nudging you to go, then you are deceiving yourself and everyone else in the process.

XO *Take a step forward on your behalf:*

You must do what is right for you, but do it with consideration and respect for everyone.

**The most beautiful and horrifying thing about the innocence of children is that they aren't afraid of strangers,
and they don't doubt that the world is benevolent.**

The sad truth about the innocence of children is that they trust and believe what they are told. Especially when they hear they are not good enough.

Anything that happened to you as an innocent child was not only **not your fault**, but it was also completely out of your control. Your survival has meaning, and you matter.

It is time to forgive ourselves for all things inflicted upon us.

XO *Take a step forward on your behalf:*

Write the letter to yourself that you waited for but didn't arrive. You know what you need to hear.

Your penmanship is powerful and your compassion more so.

IT'S TIME TO MAKE NO A PART OF YOUR VOCABULARY.

XO *Take a step forward on your behalf:*

Say it and mean it.

Every teacher matters and every student benefits from learning something new.

Every person that comes into our lives is there to support our growth. Be willing to learn from all your teachers, especially the ones you don't like. They come bearing useful offerings.

Don't overwhelm your self-forgiveness list with more regrets about missed opportunities.

Learn and grow now.

 *Take a step forward on your behalf:*

Allow yourself to hear all messages, especially the offensive ones. Everything becomes useful if we are willing to use it to serve us.

AN OPEN MIND OPENS DOORS WHILE USING IT'S POWER TO CLOSE OTHERS.

XO *Take a step forward on your behalf:*

Make room for opportunities to show up in your life. When one door opens… **close some doors.**

Give yourself limitless chances because your opportunities for happiness are limited to how much you believe you deserve.

XO *Take a step forward on your behalf:*

Make the choice today to believe in you and your worth. It is a choice.

A good sense of humor helps when it comes to forgiving ourselves for blindly trusting the people we believe are trustworthy, even when they show us they are greedy, evil liars.

Don't be swayed by a designer suit, a great education, and a stellar presentation.

Take your blinders off and recognize that you must always have your back.

Have a good laugh when you figure out that you fell for a well-designed trap and unfairly pronounced yourself more stupid than you could have ever imagined.

Acknowledge your loving heart and recognize that your trust and faith meters were turned up to maximum volume and your lie detectors were off.

 *Take a step forward on your behalf:*

Throw the benefit of the doubt out of the window and hold others accountable.

TRUST THAT THE FEELING OF NOT BELONGING IS INFORMING YOU THAT YOU WOULD BE HAPPIER SOMEWHERE ELSE.

At times we desire to be part of something so much that we are willing to feel uncomfortable to belong there.

Have faith that you are being guided and that you won't always know where you are meant to be until you arrive there.

There is a knowing in all of us that requires no questions or explanations. It is that profound.

XO Take a step forward on your behalf:

Have faith in your intuition. Allow yourself to be guided.

YOU ARE THE ONLY ONE YOU CAN TRULY COUNT ON, SO MAKE YOURSELF COUNT.

XO *Take a step forward on your behalf:*

It's time to be number one. Declare it so.

The fastest, most effective path toward self-forgiveness is by taking intentional action steps that support you. Treating yourself not only with physical and emotional care, but also honoring who you are by owning the privilege to be you and know you.

Become proud to bond with yourself deeply and to understand fully how complex and amazing you are.

Become your sacred admirer in awe of all that you are.

 Take a step forward on your behalf:

Honor yourself by doing something profoundly loving for yourself.

Imagine you are a new love interest you want to impress.

As you see you, you shall be seen.

You have full control over how others see you by the way you see yourself.

Forgive yourself for minimizing your greatness and get ready to shine.

 *Take a step forward on your behalf:*

Choose to embrace your greatness. You are a gift from God.

It's not about being your best, it's about being your friend.

XO *Take a step forward on your behalf:*

Being kind and compassionate with yourself will automatically create the positive change you would like to see. Start with acceptance. It leads to all good things.

Dear God and The Universe,

Thank you for the best day ever yesterday. It was a bit of a doozy, but I trust that as per my asking, you are showing me what I cannot yet see.

Thank you for your guidance, energy, protection, support, and love. I have faith that I will know what to do in all situations with the direction that I feel called to move in, the guidance that you send me through me. I choose not to worry anymore, as I know this doesn't bode well for me. Instead, I have strengthened my faith that you know my best path and I will feel it too. I love you more than you know. I love you more than I know. Please, send me another best day ever today. Thank you. I love you.

Every day, I pick up a bright yellow telephone that sits on an end table in my living room. It is my direct line to God and The Universe, and I start the day with a conversation. This practice sets the intention for my day, and it has changed my life. I NEVER fail to do this, and I NEVER ask *why* something happened. Such practices that are backed with intention, create magic in your life. You must add them to your life. **They support self-forgiveness to stick.**

 *Take a step forward on your behalf:*

Create a daily practice and do not deviate from it. Make sure it is something you love.

When what can never happen keeps happening, don't live in the dark any longer.

On most people's self-forgiveness list are the resentments we hold against ourselves for **being taken for a fool.**

Stop blindly trusting. Stop giving the benefit of the doubt. Stop covering your ears when the truth is too painful to bear. Stop trying to make sense out of what never made sense to begin with. Trust your gut. Do your due diligence. Take your blinders off for good.

Fools are people being foolish.

XO Take a step forward on your behalf:

Stop thinking and believing that other people would never do what you could not imagine, and stop assuming that what you think would never happen is an impossibility. Don't become the fool.

**Your journey is an adventure that is meant for you.
Learn to love your aloneness.**

XO *Take a step forward on your behalf:*

Start doing some things on your own by yourself. It's wonderful to have an experience just with you. Allow yourself to soak it in. Learn to be happy when you are by yourself. Your own company awaits you.

You don't have to change, to change your perception of you.

Instead of striving to become a better person than you already are, change the way you judge yourself and a new image will emerge.

XO *Take a step forward on your behalf:*

Self-forgiveness flows steadily as you change the way you see yourself. Write a powerful compliment about yourself and post it on your bathroom mirror.

NEVER BETRAY YOURSELF TO MAKE SOMEONE ELSE HAPPY

Choices that betray the self so that someone else can feel special or get their way, won't bode well over time.

XO *Take a step forward on your behalf:*

Make your choices count the most. It is more selfish to be inauthentic and pretend with others.

Are you certain you have what you are afraid to lose?

Do you stop to think that what you cling to so tightly may not be an accurate assessment of what is?

What if instead, you are feeling fear and desperation because you see no options or think you can't handle a situation?

Whether we like it or not, until we make the choices that best serve us, others may make them for us.

 *Take a step forward on behalf of you:*

Start taking a stand for you and make the choices that serve you.

COUNT YOUR LOSSES.
Your growth depends on it.

With all the loss you have lived through and survived will appear something to be thankful for. Even in the darkest of times, light peeks through the tiniest of openings and brings hope.

XO *Take a step forward on your behalf:*

Take some time and recall two great losses in your life. Consider how you have grown from these experiences.

Allow your past to remind you of your strength.

XO *Take a step forward on your behalf:*

Remember the first time you took a stand for yourself and how it made you feel. Writing it in your journal will help to bring it alive.

You are all you have, and you can have it all.

Once you forgive yourself, you will learn to trust and believe in you.

Once you trust and believe in you, the possibilities are endless.

XO Take a step forward on your behalf:

Start counting on yourself for all that you need.

There may be no dress rehearsals to the events of our lives, but we do gain the growth and experience to practice what we preach. Live grounded in *your* values and beliefs.

XO *Take a step forward on your behalf:* Practice what you preach and walk your talk.

KNOW YOUR NON-NEGOTIABLES AND DON'T NEGOTIATE

Self-forgiveness takes commitment, consistency, accountability, and dedication. It also requires that you keep your word to yourself.

When it comes to the promises you make on your behalf, you must do everything in your power to not falter. Each time you do, it becomes more of an uphill path.

Promises to the self, when broken, become bigger obstacles to climb. Be mindful.

 *Take a step forward on your behalf:*

Don't make promises to yourself that you know you won't keep.

YOU WERE NEVER WRONG. YOU JUST MADE THE DECISION TO MAKE EVERYONE ELSE RIGHT.

FORGIVE YOURSELF

XO *Take a step forward on your behalf:*

This one's a biggie. You must breathe and let it go. From now on, you must own your perspective and stop doubting yourself. You were always right based on your perception of things. And it is important to know that *they* were right too, based on *their* perception of things.

No matter how many times you abandon yourself, you cannot leave yourself behind.

BOND WITH AND BEFRIEND THE ONLY PERSON WHO WILL REMAIN WITH YOU FOR YOUR ENTIRE JOURNEY.

Whenever you choose it, you've got a friend.

XO *Take a step forward on your behalf:*

Meet a new friend today: **You.**

WHEREVER YOU GO, GO WITH YOU.

XO *Take a step forward on your behalf:*

Be conscious and intentional of being in your presence and consider your needs and desires as most important.

> ***It's never been about wiping the slate clean.
> That would be throwing wisdom in the trash.***

Your journey is your adventure. It is unique and it is solely yours. Your joy and sorrow make up who you are and what you become. It is your choice what you do with what is.

Self-forgiveness only becomes a process when we choose it and commit to it, not because we should, but because we desire to live a full life as we intend it.

Your heart longs for your commitment.

 *Take a step forward on your behalf:*

Be grateful for your wisdom and honor your journey. It isn't over yet.

YOUR HEART HOLDS THE SECRET TO YOUR HAPPY LIFE.

Secrets are best kept sacred.

All the information you need to live your intended life is in your possession. You needn't look further. You know all the answers to the questions you ask.

Your **gut** is your guidance, and your **heart** will steer you ahead.

 *Take a step forward on your behalf:*

Listen closely to the whisper of your heart. Heed its call.

A **Sacred Admirer** is someone who is not only in awe of oneself, but who considers their existence invaluable to the world. They understand that their purpose is specific and one that speaks to their heart while bestowing upon others the precious gifts only they can offer. A **Sacred Admirer** considers that if they were gone, their loss would be missed and mourned, not because they people-pleased or bribed others to like and approve of them, not because they sacrificed themselves and their families to show up for strangers, not because they contributed freely to the community, but instead, because their love, gratitude, and respect for themselves was so admired, envied, and desired by all. Undying belief in ourselves and our worth is what we all yearn for and it allows us to authentically reach out to others and the world in loving ways. A **Sacred Admirer** knows their value and they never question their worth.

 Take a step forward on your behalf:

Become your Sacred Admirer and watch the magic unfold. You will be kinder and more loving than you could possibly imagine now. Allow for self-actualization to begin.

HAPPY BONDING.

Do so with joy, wonder, and excitement to get to know you.

XO *Take a step forward on your behalf:*

Be your love interest and get curious about you. You are amazing.

We yearn for permission to be **selfish**;
that is why we try
so hard not to be.

We don't have the go ahead to be.

Being selfish is the only way we will fill
ourselves up
and serve the world.

Give yourself permission to be **selfish**, even for a little while. You will discover it was the missing link all along. Soon you will feel so filled up you will run out in the streets to support others.

Desire trumps obligation any day
of the week.

XO *Take a step forward on your behalf:*

Stop making selfish a dirty word and allow yourself your pleasures. Fill yourself up.

Don't leave yourself out of what you do for another.

XO *Take a step forward on your behalf:*

Attend to your own priorities first. Others can and will wait.

It's not about forgetting the past. It's about remembering your journey.

Even with the situations we wish didn't happen. Even with the circumstances we'd rather not recall. Even with all the heartache we endured. Even with the times we lost faith. It has been a journey, part of a bigger picture and a brighter path.

Don't lose sight of all the good times and memories just to highlight the darkness. Bring in the light and see the full journey. It's not over yet. Look up.

XO *Take a step forward on your behalf:*

Make a list of some very happy memories. Let some light in.

**The right thing to do, if it isn't
right for you,
is not the right thing to do.
Take your losses and stay true to you.**

XO *Take a step forward on your behalf:*

Live your truth.

Self-forgiveness and New Beginnings

At any moment, at any time, in any place, you can choose to forgive yourself, to start anew, to begin again with new faith that your life is not only on course but going somewhere exciting. And once you give yourself permission to put it all aside, to no longer hold things against you, you free yourself up to allow new opportunities to present themselves, to see the synchronicities, to read the signs and messages that guide you, to renew your trust and belief in you and what your intended life is.

Let the magic unfold!

XO Take a step forward on your behalf:

Keep breathing. Keep walking. Keep forgiving yourself for all of it.

IT'S GETTING BETTER ALL THE TIME.

A mantra to live by.

FROM MY DEAREST SELF TO YOUR DEAREST SELF,

I hope you set yourself free.

As an Emotional Wellness Coach for thirteen years, Eve supports her clients to step into their lives with both feet.

Honoring her own journey, filled with both heartache and joy, Eve knows that living one's intended life is essential to find meaning and purpose. She believes whole-heartedly that self-forgiveness is the way.

ALSO BY EVE ROSENBERG

Your Happy Life Realized: How to Stop Putting Others First and Yourself Last NOW!

Be Selfish, Eat Well, Serve Many: Taking the Path to Your Happiest Life

I Don't Want to Take Care of My Mother: How to Forgive the Woman Who Neglected You

To learn more, visit www.howtobelieveinyou.com.

www.ingramcontent.com/pod-product-compliance
Lightning Source LLC
Chambersburg PA
CBHW072209070526
44585CB00015B/1266